Dominic Salles still lives in Swindon, with his workaholic wife Deirdre. His jiu-jitsu-loving ex-engineer son, Harry, has moved to Shoreditch and lives on the site of Shakespeare's first theatre. Destiny. For those of you who remember Bob, he is now an ex-dog. It's curtains for him and The Curtain for Harry.

His daughter Jess is moving to New Zealand where the surf is better, and the rugby is better than Wales. He spent three months in Andorra this year, learning to snowboard. He is not as cool as he thinks, but he will spend part of the summer in New Zealand snowboarding on a volcano.

His sister Jacey is an actress, famous for her Spanish accent, on your TV screens in shows like Casualty and Cold Feet. She would be hilarious in her own YouTube channel. Tweet her to let her know.

His YouTube channel, Mr Salles Teaches English, has reached 100,000 subscribers, about which he is childishly excited. 30% of his viewers said they improved by at least 3 grades in 2022.

He drives a Toyota Prius and is getting solar panels this year to offset his enormous carbon footprint. I don't expect they will fit on the car though.

Other Grade 9 Guides by Mr Salles

Language

The Mr Salles Guide to **100% at AQA GCSE English Language**
The Mr Salles Guide to **Awesome Story Writing**
The Mr Salles Quick Guide to **Awesome Description**
The Mr Salles **Ultimate Guide to Description**
The Mr Salles Quick **Guide to Grammar, Punctuation and Spelling**
The Mr Salles **Ultimate Guide to Persuasive Writing**
The Mr Salles Guide to 100% in AQA GCSE **English Language Paper 1 Question 2**
The Mr Salles Guide to 100% in AQA GCSE **English Language Paper 1 Question 3**
The Mr Salles Guide to 100% in AQA GCSE **English Language Paper 1 Question 4**
The Mr Salles Guide to 100% in AQA GCSE **English Language Paper 1 Question 5**
The Mr Salles Guide to 100% in AQA GCSE **English Language Paper 2 Question 2**

Literature

The Mr Salles Guide to **GCSE English Literature**
Study Guide Mr Salles Analyses **Jekyll and Hyde**
The Mr Salles Ultimate Guide to **Macbeth**

The Mr Salles Guide to **An Inspector Calls**

The Mr Salles Ultimate Guide to **A Christmas Carol**

The Mr Salles Ultimate Guide to **Romeo and Juliet**

Mr Salles **Power and Conflict** Top Grade Essay Guide (AQA Anthology): 11 Grade 9 Exam Essays!

Books on Teaching

The Full English: How to be a brilliant English teacher

The Slightly Awesome Teacher: Using Edu-research to get brilliant results

The Unofficial Ofsted Survival Guide

Differentiate Your School: where every student learns more

Contents

AQA Language Paper 2
Question 2

What Do You Need to Do?

The question will ask you to write about something both texts have in common. Both texts in paper 2 will be about the same topic.

The question will take *part* of that topic. Let's imagine the two texts were both about tennis matches. The question will take part of the match – the final games, or the winning players, or the losing players, or the lines people, or the role of the crowd – whatever, something which is in both texts, but in **parts** of it.

This is because the examiners want you to prove that you can find relevant information.

In theory, the examiners could ask you to find similarities and differences. For example, "**write a summary of the similarities and differences** of the winning players of both matches."

But instead, they will almost definitely ask you to write about only *one* of these, *just* the similarities or *just* the differences. This is because the examiners want you to have to find most of the information for full marks.

For example, there might be only 5 possible quotations to compare in each text, and you would need to find 4 from each to get full marks.

What is a Summary

This means: cut out the fluff, cut to the chase, just give me the facts…

The most fool proof way of doing this is to answer in numbered points. No one does this in the exam, because teachers train you to write in paragraphs. I also write in paragraphs, and I also used to train my students to write in paragraphs for this question in the exam.

But after reading and writing over 100 answers to this question, I realise it is far easier to force the examiner to give you marks this way (starting a new line for each point).

Let's imagine the question is:

> **Use details from both sources to write a summary of what you understand about the differences between the players who win both tennis matches.**

The Salles Method

1. In Source A the winning player feels X (insert quote to prove).
2. *From this we can infer Y.*
3. However, in Source B the winning player is different. She feels A (insert quote to prove)

4. ***From this we can infer Z.***
5. Repeat until you have made 4 comparisons, and made 8 inferences.

In all the answers, look out for the text in bold italic. This is always where the student is showing their inference.

How This is Marked

The mark scheme is full of abstract ideas, which make it very tricky to use:

Level 1: **Simple**: limited summary 1–2 marks

Level 2: **Some**: attempts at summary 3–4 marks

Level 3: **Clear**: relevant summary 5–6 mark

Level 4: **Perceptive**: detailed summary 7–8 marks

But how do you decide what 'simple' looks like compared to 'some'? What 'clear' looks like, compared to 'perceptive'? What 'relevant' looks like compared to 'detailed'?

And then, how do you make sure that your decisions are the same as your teacher's? And how does your teacher make sure that their decision is the same as an examiner? And how does the examiner make sure their decision is the same as a senior examiner?

Well, the answer is, you can't.

Ofqual, who regulate the exam boards, have found you can't get examiners to fully agree on a mark in any subject, and that the subject with least agreement is English. Yes, GCSE exam marking is a lottery, and most dodgy of these lotteries is English. Let me show you what this means:

So, examiners are allowed to disagree by at least 1 mark on this question, and Ofqual and AQA say that's perfectly fine. Because there are only 8 marks, but 9 GCSE grades, 1 mark is ***at least*** 1 grade different! Yes, it is totally ok for the examiner to give you the wrong grade, as long as it is only 1 grade out, rather than 2.

That's Why the Salles Method Works

The method makes it almost impossible for the examiner to give you the wrong grade.

- Points 1 and 3 give you a comparison, with a quote as evidence. **1 mark.**
- Points 2 and 4 give you an explanation of the quotations in 1 and 3. **1 mark.**
- Do the same for the next two quotations that show your similarity or difference. **2 more marks.**
- Do the same for the next two quotations that show your similarity or difference. **2 more marks.**
- Do the same for the next two quotations that show your similarity or difference. **2 more marks.**

Question finished!

Based on AQA Paper 2 November 2021

Source A

This extract is from Dominic Salles' autobiography, published in 2023. Here, he writes about the different forms of sweets and sugar based treats children would eat in Ibiza in the 1970s.

Each day on the island was an adventure, a dozen children roaming each of its four corners. The summer stretched out far and wide, and further still.

The Golden Bull kids would meet with the Piccadilly Bar kids and the two would combine and greet the Maruka Bar kids and then they would swallow up the kids from the other beaches, all our territories from Figueretas to Playa d'en Bossa, where the hotels stopped.

In season, the sands were scorching. The tiled pavements and pool sides were cooking-hot: blisters would catch you, if your feet weren't flying. We ran and played on dirt tracks all summer, and all year round our feet were tougher than hide so we could almost tread on sea urchins without pain.

At the movies all of us hoarded salted sun-flower seeds, or Pipas. Pipas were cracked and their shells spat out, the Spanish way of creating the noises that the English produce more quietly by unwrapping sweets and chocolate. Pipas were cheaper than chips and all of us could afford a full bag, spitting shells out onto the floor, on seat backs and any enemies in the row in front.

Every Christmas, without fail, we all gorged ourselves on turron. One type was a brick of thick, hard and stubborn nougat cement, encasing almonds. So brittle was the nougat that it could crack milk teeth, and once bitten shattered like white marble. It was like biting a plate. The peanut turrones were soft and warm, wet and slick with oil. Imagine chewing peanut butter which suddenly turns to liquid and dribbles down your chin.

Ensaimadas came in wonderful flavours, frosted with powdered sugar like a gateway drug. We could have them filled with cream, apricot or chocolate and the filling would explode unpredictably as you bit in – hence the fun of eating them. The ensaimada was a pastry half way between a doughnut and a croissant, as addictive as an aged whiskey. My parents fed them to me for breakfast in a pit stop on the way to school.

Chupa-Chups were the longest lasting treat, a lollipop. You could suck on one for most of a film, its stick poking out of your lips while the roof of your mouth cut itself on the sharp ridges of boiled sugar. If you dared to chew, you knew fillings were being carved out of your molars, rather than through the slow work of constantly sucking sugar.

Churros were the most addictive treat, even more of a masterpiece than ensaimadas. A churro was a long, thick, ridged rope of doughnut, deep fried and sugared, each ridge a triangle to double the surface area. This was their brilliant design for dipping in hot chocolate or caramel sauces: in cross-section they looked like stars and they tasted of heaven.

There were two ways to eat these, balancing greed and sociability. You could horde the churros, twirling them into the chocolate sauce, scooping ever thicker layers of dark splendour, before twirling the end into your drooling mouth, spinning them to keep the sauce from dripping.

Or you could invite a friend to join you and elegantly take turns, dipping only the ends in sauce, and sharing the lasting pleasure, while you gazed into the eyes of the girl you were treating, or frowning at the boy who was scooping far too much of your share. Buzzing with sugar, we'd run down to the beach and plunge into the waters, our eyes immune to the stinging salt, while our teeth silently rotted.

I'd had seven fillings by the time I was ten, none with anaesthetic. I hadn't made the connection between my sugar addiction and the dentist's drill. Rather than change my diet, my mother introduced me to whiskey aged seven, like a medicine to dull the post-dentist pain.

This is an extract from a magazine article written in 1870. The writer describes candy being made in the little known European country called Monteblanco.

As they clutch at their candy so greedily, no child asks how the sweet was made. Yet the creation of these treats – or perhaps I mean addictions – of childhood is a subject for analysis.

A great reversal has changed society's attitudes regarding candy and treats of every kind. Once parents demonised them as "ungodly temptations" and, just like forbidden fruits, children sought them out even more eagerly.

Well, far be it from me to denounce these sugary delights that make children's mouths drool. Savoured moderately, few things are more beneficial than honey. Being packed with carbohydrates, it both warms and nourishes the body.

In previous generations, candy was uncommon in Monteblanco; there was no manufacturing of candy in huge factories. All the supply of quality candy originated from Italy and France but the great advances in steam-powered machinery have made Monteblanco the world's prime producer of candy. Sweets are now both cheaper and widely available.

The unimaginative ideas of the past have been swept away. Now customers taste with their eyes as well as tongues, even sweets which cost little. Imagine a penny's worth of candy packaged in a red-ribboned wrapper.

True enough, a few of the showiest candies of the past were beautiful, but the colours were made from lead based paints, and this metal is wickedly poisonous. The renowned Professor Vassall's testing of this virulently coated candy, over a decade ago, laid bare the terrible practice of luring our little ones with paint made from poisons.

The more colourful the coating, the more poisonous the candy. Vibrant colours decorating your confectionary were probably poisons containing copper.

Small wonder candies were condemned when they were so toxic. Indeed one might speculate than many infants were killed by gorging themselves on such beautifully painted sweets.

Professor Vassal has valiantly saved us from this terrible threat to our much-loved little ones. Colours now are extracted from plants and vegetables and, if not as dazzling as those toxic metals, they are perfectly healthy.

Although today's confections are free from toxins, take care. It may still be that some old toxic stock of candy may yet be sold, so I urge parents to reject candy coated with vibrant primary colours as potential poisons.

Candy factories mainly employs girls. Though they work quickly and with great concentration, they are young; candy and hungry bellies both cause temptation, and these young girls are tempted.

Rather than pay higher wages, the girls are free to eat as much candy as they wish, and indeed this is used as justification for reduced pay. In the workplace I investigated, these young girls appeared not to suffer from their addiction to sugar, and their farm fed cheeks certainly disproved any fear of candy's dangers.

These tiny women-to-be make the candies with urgency, quietly hunching over their work stations. In a further backroom, I found young artists painstakingly painting tiny candy treats under the authoritarian gaze of their managers.

All the colours were plant based and perfectly safe. The colouring requires little skill and the girls are too poorly paid to take proper care. Yet, though the candy is not a form of art, each sweet is a morsel of goodness. How different this is from the recent yet poisonous past.

Professor Vassal has indeed been a police inspector of our health and a saviour of our children.

Question 2

You need to refer to **Source A** and **Source B** for this question.

The boys and girls in Ibiza in **Source A** and girls making candy in **Source B** have different experiences.

Use details from **both** sources to write a summary of what you understand about the different experiences all the children had.

8 marks

My Response 1

1. The kids in Source A travelled to Ibiza. They bought candy.

2. In Monteblanco the kids visited the movies. They ate sweets and watched the films.

3. The girls in Source B lived in Monteblanco. There weren't any big industries there.

4. The girls in the sweet factories *are bored because the factories have very little to do*.

1 mark

Examiner Comments

- There is only one relevant comparison, which we have to work out. The girls work in a factory in Source B. In source A children go to the movies. **1 mark**.
- All the rest is either not a comparison, or factually wrong.

My Response 2

1. The boys and girls in Source A and the girls in Source B lead lives which are both different and similar.

2. Evidence for this is in Source A, "At the movies all of us hoarded salted sun-flower seeds".

3. This differs from Source B where the girls are only permitted to eat plant based food. Evidence for this is "extracted from plants and vegetables."

4. *These show the difference that the children didn't have similar freedoms to eat the same foods.*

2 marks

Examiner Comments

- Point 1 does not make a comparison. **Zero marks.**
- Point 2 compares with point 3. **1 mark.**
- Point 4 contains an explanation for both points 2 and 3. **1 mark.**

My Response 3

1. *The boys and girls in Source A seem to be having fun. They are all happy because they all eat sweets, which is a good thing.*

2. *However, the girls are not happy in Source B. This is because they spend so long working for very low pay.*

3. The girls eat the candy they make because "candy and hungry bellies both cause temptation".

4. This is a contrast to the kids in Source A.

5. Overall, these kids enjoy life and are filled with happiness, whereas the girls are not.

3 marks

Examiner Comments

- Point 1 is compared with point 2, for **1 mark.**
- Both points include an explanation. **1 mark.**
- Point 3 is compared, just about, to point 4 – it is implied that in Source A the children don't make their own sweets. **1 mark.**
- Point 5 compares the children in both sources. But it is not a new comparison, it just sums up what has already been written. **Zero marks.**

My Response 4

1. Dominic Salles gives a fun-filled account of being a child, emphasising "At the movies all of us hoarded salted sun-flower seeds, or Pipas", *which highlights the enjoyment of childhood as the children eat together.*

2. However, in Source B *we see the sadness of the girls' lives being forced to work*, "Candy factories mainly employs girls".

3. In Source B "the girls are free to eat as much candy as they wish" *which reveals how their health is not looked after and their employers are not compassionate*.

4. However, in Source A Dominic *shows that the girls and boys have an enjoyable childhood*, "we'd run down to the beach and plunge into the waters".

5. Dominic also emphasises the sensations of the treats they ate, "The peanut turrones were soft and warm, wet and slick with oil".

4 marks

Examiner Comments

- Points 1 and 2 are a comparison. **1 mark.**
- Each of points 1 and 2 have an explanation of what this reveals about the children's experience. **1 mark.**
- Points 3 and 4 are a comparison. **1 mark.**
- Each of points 3 and 4 have an explanation of what this reveals about the children's experience. **1 mark.**
- Point 5 is not a comparison of the childhood experiences. **Zero marks.**

My Response 5

1. In Source A *the children enjoy being children*. They go to the beach and swim, "Buzzing with sugar, we'd run down to the beach and plunge into the waters".

2. In contrast in Source B the "the girls are too poorly paid" *so they are poor. The factory owners do this deliberately*, "the girls are free to eat as much candy as they wish, and indeed this is used as justification for reduced pay".

3. In Source A, the children would meet up in a large group, coming from all the bars. The beach was scorching.

4. But in Source B *the girls are closely watched*, "quietly hunching over their work stations... under the authoritarian gaze of their managers." *This shows that the conditions of their work are unhappy, and this unhappiness is made worse by the poor wages.*

4 marks

Examiner Comments

- Points 1 and 2 are a comparison: **1 mark.**
- Each comparison has an explanation about the children's experience. **1 mark.**
- Points 3 and 4 are set out like a comparison, although how point 3 relates to point 4 is not well explained. The examiner would want to give this half a mark, but half a mark is not permitted, so they have decided on **1 mark.**
- Point 3 has no explanation of the experience of childhood, but point 4 has two in total: **1 mark.**

My Response 6

1. The children in Source A *were united in play* and being able to go to the cinema.

2. *They had freedom*, "We ran and played on dirt tracks all summer".

3. *They had leisure to discover* "two ways to eat these, [treats] balancing greed and sociability".

4. *Their families could also afford to buy them all treats at Christmas*, "Every Christmas, without fail, we all gorged ourselves on turron".

5. They used treats as a way to make friends, "Or you could invite a friend to join you and elegantly take turns" eating churros.

6. This paints a picture of a happy childhood, where children enjoy each other's company and have fun filled activities.

7. However, in Source B, the girls have "hungry bellies".

8. They are also "largely employed" **rather than free to have fun**.

9. Although the girls were also able to eat lots of sweets, **this was possibly instead of real food**.

5 marks

Examiner Comments

- The comparisons don't begin until point 7. Points 7, 8 and 9 are each comparisons with any or all of the points 1-6. So, there are 3 comparisons for **3 marks**.
- There are lots of explanations about the experiences of childhood for Source A, but only two for Source B, in points 8 and 9. Every time there is an explanation for Source A and another for Source B, we can award 1 mark. So, this scores **2 marks**.
- You can see that this student could easily have scored more marks by organising their writing so that each point made about Source A was compared to Source B.
- In other words, if the student had used the Salles Method I set out at the beginning, they would have scored many more marks.

My Response 7

1. The kids in Source A "ran and played on dirt tracks all summer".

2. **We can infer that their lives were carefree.**

3. **And there was no requirement for them to find jobs as children.**

4. However, in Source B the girls are made to work in factories.

5. This **experience is made worse as** they receive "reduced pay".

6. In Source A, the children **lead happy and enjoyable lives**.

7. And **they don't have any restrictions placed on them**.

8. Whereas in Source B **the girls have been robbed of their childhood**.

9. **They work very long hours, which we infer** from how they are "quietly hunching over their work stations".

10. They also work "under the authoritarian gaze of their managers" **so we can infer that their working conditions are harsh**.

6 marks

Examiner Comments

- Point 1 compares with point 4. **1 mark.**
- Points 1 and 4 don't contain an explanation about the experiences of childhood. **Zero marks.**
- Point 2 compares with point 8. **1 mark.**
- Each point contains an explanation. **1 mark.**
- Point 5 compares with point 7. **1 mark.**
- Each point contains an explanation. **1 mark.**
- Point 6 compares with point 9. **1 mark.**
- However, point 6 and point 2 are very similar. So really, this on its own would probably have scored zero marks. However, point 10 is another comparison to point 6. So, one way or another, the comparison should score a mark. But it doesn't – see below.
- There are not enough separate explanations about Source A. This therefore can't be treated as "perceptive inferences from **both** texts".
- In other words, you can't just keep making inferences about one text. For each inference, you want to compare it to the other text.
- Once again, you can see how following the Salles Method would have forced the student to keep making an equal number of comparisons from both sources, and they would likely have scored 8/8.

My Response 8

1. Source A **portrays the children as spoilt and unruly, which we can infer from** "spitting shells out onto the floor, seat backs and any enemies". **This portrays the children behaving badly.**

2. **It also shows that they are spoilt, feeling entitled to misbehave in this way.**

3. **We can see this same lack of control** at Christmas when "we all gorged ourselves on turron".

4. **This also suggests they take treats for granted and are a bit ungrateful.**

5. Source A **portrays childhood as being a period without responsibility.**

6. Source B **shows that children in the nineteenth century were not as free.**

7. These girls had jobs and responsibilities, as "Candy factories mainly employs girls" rather than adults.

8. **This reveals that these girls did not have the luxuries** of the children in Source A.

9. **This also implies that the girls lived in poverty, which is why they felt forced into work.**

10. **We can also infer this poverty from the girls having** "hungry bellies".

11. Unlike the children in Source A, who eat treats in addition to a normal diet, the girls in Source B eat sweets instead of proper food.

12. Because we know "they are young" *we can infer that society at the time found this child labour was socially acceptable.*

7 marks

Examiner Comments

- Point 2 compares with point 8. **1 mark.**
- Each point contains an explanation. **1 mark.**
- Point 3 compares with point 11. **1 mark.**
- Point 3 contains an explanation, but point 11 doesn't. **Zero marks.**
- Point 4 compares with point 10. **1 mark.**
- Each point contains an explanation. **1 mark.**
- Point 5 compares with point 6. **1 mark.**
- Each point contains an explanation. **1 mark.**
- Points 7, 9 and 12 are all excellent inferences, but they are not linked to a comparison. **Zero marks.**
- As you can see, it is difficult for the examiner to work out what the comparisons are because students tend to set their answers out in an unhelpful way. This is why you should consider the Salles Method.
- If you set out your answers with a point about Source A, and then an immediate similarity or difference in Source B, it will be much easier for the examiner to mark. Doing this would have made it impossible for this student not to gain full marks.

Based on AQA Paper 2 November 2020

Source A

Source A is an extract from a book, The Abyss Stares Back at You. Ben Youngs and Jack Van Portvliet are experienced climbers. They have just climbed K2, a 28,000 foot tall mountain in the Himalayas. On the way down, Ben broke his leg. In this extract, Ben describes how Jack had to lower him down the mountain.

The ridge was freezing in the wind. Below us sat the blue glacier we'd climbed just a week ago. It snaked down to base camp, about a 4000 foot descent from us. It would be hard and Jack would need all his strength to keep lowering me, but at least the despair we'd both felt when my leg broke had vanished.

"It's getting dark," Jack said.

I watched Jack calculating probabilities. I said nothing. I wanted to continue. But Jack was sacrificing his safe descent to help me. I had to let him decide.

"Let's do it," he said.

Jack fed the rope quicker than before, and I cried out in fear and pain as I slid down the mountain. But he kept up the same pace. After 20 meters, I stopped shouting. The mounting wind and the sound of small avalanches on the ridge drowned out my yells. I just focused on my broken left leg to stop it catching in the snow. It was hopeless. Though I lay on my right side, my left boot kept bouncing into the snow and catching as my whole bodyweight pushed downward. Each snagging stabbed and burned with pain. I cried out and tried not to scream, cursed the weather and the mountain, and cursed Jack loudest of all.

Then we'd stop while he climbed down to me. I would put my weight on my right leg and try to focus on my breathing to ease the pain. Gradually, my mind began to clear. The pain throbbed instead of stabbing, and my whole body begged to rest and sleep.

My descent started once more, and beyond trying to help myself I let myself fall. My leg screamed with pain, and I longed for an unconsciousness which did not come. I yelled and begged Jack to stop; he didn't and I yelled curses and accusations at him as though he was deliberately torturing me.

The descent stopped, and I braced myself on the rope. Jack tugged four times, the signal for me to hop onto my left leg. I sank beneath a sea of pain. I pressed my face into the mountain and let the freezing snow bite at cheeks to distract me from my agony. Once more, the stabbing pain ebbed and my mind began to recover. My knee was much worse now, and several times I'd heard bone or tendon or both tear or snap. Each time it snagged more damage was done. Tears froze on my face.

I couldn't control how my leg shook. I shoved my face into the icy snow and waited. The throbbing and shaking eased. At last, I could hear Jack descending. I couldn't see him, far above me.

Once more I dug a ledge into the ice and snow. Jack would sit here to lower me. I began to sweat from work rather than pain. I looked up and made Jack out, climbing down rapidly towards me.

He was cheerful. "We're making great time," he said.

"Yes, great time," I said. There was no point screaming at him now.

He readied himself on the ledge, ready to belay*, his hands gripping the rope.

"You're in a hurry," I said.

"Quite fancy a brew, Ben. Let's go."

He smiled and his humour gave me confidence. No soldier left behind, I mused. This was a rescue, and rather than climbing partners, we were now comrades. The accident had happened, but we'd simply shifted focus. Move forward, think positively, work as a team.

"I'll brew it myself," I said, positioning my good side on the slope. "Go slower in case this leg snaps off."

But I might as well have said nothing, because Jack tossed me downward even faster than last time, and the waves of agony overwhelmed me, submerging me in pain. My confidence vanished.

Glossary

* to belay – a metal clip is hammered into the mountain, and Jack can pass the rope through it to lower Ben.

Source B

In 1898, English adventurer Ursula Bear climbs the highest mountain in the Alps, Mont Blanc. This source is an extract from a letter to her mother describing her climb.

Sunday, 12th August 1898.

No doubt you surmised from my previous correspondence that I was determined to climb Mont Blanc, and have been awaiting news of my safe descent. But I must declare – it is terrifying. If I had understood the challenge which faced me, I would have declined to meet it, but I was ignorant of the difficulties, and now look upon it with utmost delight – I imagine myself ready to meet all future challenges...

I set off on Saturday, hiring a local, Hugo, to be my guide and we climbed to the mountain hut. From there, I marvelled at the gorgeous sunset illuminating the glacier and granite above. Mont Blanc appeared formidable as light fell. I returned to the mountain hut, where Hugo had generously prepared a bed of straw for my blanket, and had folded my cloak into a makeshift pillow. It was a surprisingly soft bed.

We slept only till midnight, though I didn't feel rested. We washed in the river. The night was clear, with a perfect view of stars and moon. As the moon climbed the valley, so did we. Hugo went before me always, a lamp lighting the way till we reached the glacier, when the moon's light was enough, reflecting on the snow.

Ninety minutes later we took out our ropes to brave the glacier. It was a gentle cold and our breath steamed as the wind was low. For three hours, our path was mainly rock, an easy climb. My spirits lifted. But too soon, my spirits crashed! Ahead lay another three hours of very challenging slope. Twice Hugo had to use the ropes, and hauled me up like cargo.

He is as strong as a giant. If he had dropped me, or I had fallen, certain death awaited. For nearly an hour, I climbed without hope of summiting. I looked up and couldn't imagine that I wouldn't lose my footing on the rock. I confess now, I had no experience of rock climbing. Yet, I did not confess this to Hugo, and I soon shrugged off fears as I dangled above an abyss by my fingernails.

We basked at the summit till noon. A cloudless sky gave us a breath taking view. The sun warmed me as I took a thirty minute nap. Then we were ready for the descent, which was even more challenging than the climb, unless we followed the route taken by Hugo's ice axe. The cord to his wrist snapped and the axe spun away into the abyss.

Now we came to the most dangerous obstacle on Mont Blanc. Hugo leapt up, our rope in a huge coil on his back. After a time, I felt three gentle jerks on my end. "Miss Bear," he commanded and I dutifully obeyed. I found two tiny hand holds and swung out on an overhanging ledge. I dangled in mid-air while Hugo clung resolutely to his end of the rope ... one miss-step from disaster. Yet I reflected on how well the descent was going, congratulated myself on my new skills, and marvelled at my lack of fear.

We triumphed over the worst. Now came the tedious part of the descent. There were no obstacles, but one lapse of concentration could still lead to a fall and possible death. For an hour we climbed down the ice and rock face until, by good fortune, Hugo and I reached the glacier.

When we finally reached the hotel, all the staff and guests were waiting for me. The hotel owner let off fireworks at the front steps, to my delight.

I lay on my bed and unconsciousness took me till dawn, when I awoke and drank half a dozen cups of tea, then read your letters to me and slept again until mid-day. My tiredness has left me, but the muscles of my upper body feel exceedingly sore, and my knees are marvellously bruised.

Question 2

You need to refer to Source A **and** Source B for this question.

Both writers have companions during their climb: Jack in Source A and Hugo in Source B.

Use details from **both** sources to write a summary of the differences between Jack and Hugo.

8 marks

My Response 1

1. Jack and Hugo are not very alike. ***Hugo helps out Ursula.***

2. However, Ben said about Jack, "***I yelled curses and accusations at him as though he was deliberately torturing me***".

3. ***Jack seems to enjoy this torture because "He smiled … his humour".***

2 marks

Examiner Comments

- Point 1 is a comparison with point 2. **1 mark.**
- Points 2 and 3 both explain the comparison. **1 mark.**

My Response 2

1. Jack helped Ben down the slope, lowering him with ropes, so Ben "cried out in fear and pain".

2. Jack had to help Ben when Ben was injured on the descent.

3. However, in Source B, Hugo "a local" is Ursula's guide.

4. ***This implies that Hugo used his local knowledge to climb Mont Blanc and prevented Ursula from being injured.***

5. In comparison, Jack was just a friend, and not a local.

3 marks

Examiner Comments

- Point 1 is not a comparison, nor an explanation about a comparison. **Zero marks.**
- Point 2 is a comparison with point 4. **1 mark.**
- Point 3 is a comparison with point 5. **1 mark.**

- Point 4 contains an explanation of what is implied in Source B. The students does not have an explanation for Source A. Half marks can't be given. But, 2 marks for the whole answer is described as "**Simple**: limited summary". The examiner has decided that "simple" answers don't have inference. So, the extra explanation isn't treated as zero marks. Instead, it is treated as "**Some**: attempts at summary". **1 mark.**

My Response 3

1. Jack is presented as a poor companion, whereas Hugo is a good companion.

2. We can see that Jack must have done something wrong because Ben "yelled curses and accusations" at Jack.

3. However, in Source B, Hugo "hauled me up like cargo". **This simile reveals that Hugo is a kind companion.**

4. In contrast, Jack isn't kind to Ben when Jack says, "I cried out in fear and pain as I slid down the mountain. But he kept up the same pace."

5. Ben only cares about himself.

6. In contrast, Hugo is heroic, which we see when Ursula describes him "as strong as a giant".

4 marks

Examiner Comments

- Point 1 is a comparison. However, it is a general comparison which summarises what we find out in the two specific comparisons which follow. **Zero marks.**
- Points 2 and 6 are a comparison. **1 mark.**
- They both contain an explanation. **1 mark.**
- Point 3 and 4 are a comparison. **1 mark.**
- They both contain an explanation. **1 mark.**
- Point 5 is not a new comparison, and is therefore treated as part of point 4, which has already received the mark. **Zero marks.**

My Response 4

1. **Jack appears not to have any sympathy for Ben and the pain he is feeling.**

2. **We can infer this** from "I cried out in fear and pain as I slid down the mountain. But he kept up the same pace".

3. **This suggests Jack has no interest in Ben's pain and suffering.**

4. **Whereas Hugo appears to be much more considerate of Ursula.**

5. She explains that "Twice Hugo had to use the ropes, and hauled me up like cargo." *This reveals that he goes to great lengths to help his companion, unlike Jack.*

6. *Jack is also selfish in forcing Ben to descend first even though he is injured*, "I looked up and made Jack out, climbing down rapidly towards me."

7. Jack only follows Ben once he has had to descend, even with the discomfort of a broken leg.

8. This appears to be the opposite of Hugo who "went before me always, a lantern lighting the way".

9. *This makes him a much better companion than Jack.*

5 marks

Examiner Comments

- Point 3 is compared to point 4. **1 mark.**
- Both points contain an explanation. **1 mark.**
- (Points 1 and 2 are not a separate comparison, but very good explanations of point 3. There are no extra marks for this. The students should instead have made a new comparison to gain another mark). Following the Salles Method would have helped here.
- Point 5 is compared to point 6. **1 mark.**
- Both points contain an explanation. **1 mark.**
- Point 7 is compared to point 8. **1 mark.**
- Points 7 and 8 contain no explanations. **Zero marks.**
- Point 9 contains an explanation. But it is really the same explanation, though in different words, as in point 6. **Zero marks.**

My Response 5

1. *Jack is portrayed as positive and capable, even though they are facing possible tragedy.*

2. *We see his positivity when* "He was cheerful. "We're making great time," he said."

3. *This also implies a sense of humour because they must be going quite slowly as Ben is only using one leg.*

4. *His positivity is contrasted with the negative situation.*

5. In Source B Hugo is local, unlike Jack.

6. *But like Jack, Hugo is very capable.*

7. *Hugo is a master of his environment and enjoys mountain climbing.*

8. He is very strong, as Ursula reveals "He is as strong as a giant".

9. *However, Hugo appears to be more skilled than Jack*.

10. He barely speaks, *which gives him a sense of mystery*.

11. This contrasts with *Jack's sense of humour*.

5 marks

Examiner Comments

- Here we can clearly see that exam technique is crucial. Writing about one character in their entirety and then writing about the second one is a very risky strategy. It means that it is almost inevitable that you won't be writing proper comparisons. You'll forget to compare each point, as this student has done.
- Again, this is why I recommend the Salles Method instead.
- Point 5 is a comparison. **1 mark**.
- Point 6 is a comparison, but it is a similarity, rather than a difference. **Zero marks**.
- Point 9 is a comparison. **1 mark**.
- Point 10 compares with point 11. **1 mark**.
- Points 2 and 3 are an explanation to point 11. Point 10 is just about an explanation. **1 mark**.
- Points 1 and 4 are both one half of a new comparison, with two explanations about Jack. Half marks can't be awarded, but the examiner has to decide if the whole answer is "**Some**: attempts at summary" or "**Clear**: relevant summary". Both points and explanations are clearly relevant, even though they are not a full comparisons. So the examiner rounds up. **1 mark**.

My Response 6

1. *Jack appears to be a cheerful companion, which we infer from* "He was cheerful. "We're making great time," he said."

2. *He is able to remain positive even though they are facing real dangers on the mountain*.

3. *Jack is an optimist*.

4. *In contrast, Hugo is very commanding, as he works professionally*, "he commanded and I dutifully obeyed".

5. *He is also kind*: "Hugo had generously prepared a bed of straw".

6. *Unlike Jack, Hugo doesn't appear to be particularly "cheerful" or optimistic, as he is simply working on a normal day*.

7. *We can infer that he does not reveal his emotions, and therefore he is difficult for Ursula to get to know him*.

8. *Jack appears to be impatient, as Ben comments* "You're in a hurry." *He also wants to get them out of danger as quickly as possible*.

9. *In contrast, Hugh is less urgent, and takes a logical and measured approach.* We see this when "Hugo went before me always, a lamp lighting the way."

10. *This reveals how Hugo plans carefully before each climb.*

6 marks

Examiner Comments

- Point 4 is set up as a comparison with points 1, 2 and 3, using the words "in contrast". In truth, noticing that Hugo is an optimist only works as a comparison if the student comments on how Jack is either also an optimist, a pessimist, or a realist. But, the examiner will take pity on you for using a made up comparison like this, as they are not allowed to award half marks. So, **1 mark.**
- Point 4 and the earlier points all include an explanation. **1 mark.**
- Point 5 is a comparison with point 6. **1 mark.**
- They both include an explanation. **1 mark.**
- Point 7 is a great explanation. But it is not part of a comparison. **Zero marks.**
- Points 8 and 9 are a comparison. **1 mark.**
- They both include an explanation. **1 mark.**
- Point 10 is a valid explanation of the comparison in points 8 and 9. As it is not part of a new comparison, it scores nothing. **Zero marks.**
- This student would have scored 8/8 using the Salles Method!

My Response 7

1. *Jack is very thoughtful about how to help Ben in the descent. He makes difficult decisions to help them both.*

2. *We can see this thoughtfulness when* Ben "watched Jack calculating probabilities".

3. *Jack also displays leadership, which we see when* Ben observes "I had to let him decide".

4. *We can compare this to Hugo in Source B who helps Ursula, is kind towards her and is also thoughtful.*

5. *We see this kindness when* "Hugo had generously prepared a bed of straw for my blanket", *placing Ursula's comfort above his own.*

6. *This is in contrast to Jack who entirely ignores Ben's pain,* "But I might as well have said nothing, because Jack tossed me down the even faster than last time".

7. *We can infer that Jack doesn't worry about Ben's pain because he needs Ben to overcome it if they are to descend in time.*

8. *Hugo also prioritises Ursula's needs, which we see when* he "hauled me up like cargo."

9. *In contrast, Jack apparently ignores Ben's feelings and requests:* "I yelled and begged Jack to stop; he didn't".

10. *However, Hugo is far more considerate as he is gentle with her*: "I felt three gentle jerks on my end. "Miss Bear," he commanded and I dutifully obeyed."

7 marks

Examiner Comments

- Point 4 is a comparison to points 1, 2 and 3. **1 mark.**
- They include explanations. **1 mark.**
- Point 5 is compared to point 6. **1 mark.**
- They both include an explanation. **1 mark.**
- Point 8 is compared to point 9. **1 mark.**
- They both include an explanation. **1 mark.**
- Point 7 is an explanation for the comparison in point 9, and the comparison in point 6 so doesn't earn any extra marks. It would need to explain a new comparison. **Zero marks.**
- Point 10 introduces a new comparison, and it contains an explanation. However, it doesn't make a new point about Jack that hasn't been made before. The examiner can't award half marks. When added to the explanation in point 7, the examiner is persuaded to award a mark. They do this by going to the marking criteria and asking, does this help the answer become "perceptive" and "detailed", or is it still just "clear" and "relevant"? They've decided on perceptive and detailed. **1 mark.**
- As you can see, marking points 7 and 10 has been messy and difficult. If the student had simply followed the Salles Method, making points 7 and 10 a new comparison, they would have scored 8/8.

My Response 8

1. *Jack displays resilience and strength.*

2. *Jack is decisive and leads by making the critical decisions*: "I wanted to continue. But Jack was sacrificing his safe descent to help me. I had to let him decide."

3. *Ben defers to him because Jack is a good leader.*

4. *In contrast, Hugo is much more gentle than Jack, as he goes out of his way to make the climb more comfortable for Ursula.*

5. *For example, we see his kindness when,* "Hugo had generously prepared a bed of straw for my blanket".

6. *We can infer from this that Hugo and Ursula have a close bond.*

7. *Although Jack is also attentive, he is ruthless in ignoring Ben's pain.*

8. *Jack also acts urgently in the face of danger,* "I looked up and made Jack out, climbing down rapidly towards me." *He is not put off by the challenge.*

9. *He is also determined to rescue Ben, and confident that he can do so*: "He smiled and his humour gave me confidence."

10. *In contrast, Hugo is willing to take risks in order to help Ursula. We can infer that he risks his own life when* "I dangled in mid-air while Hugo clung resolutely to his end of the rope … one miss-step from disaster".

11. *Hugo also has a similar strength and bravery to Jack, which we also see when* "Twice Hugo had to use the ropes, and hauled me up like cargo."

12. *In conclusion, both companions take care of their fellow climbers. Hugo is gentle and strong. Whereas Jack is focused and strong.*

8 marks

Examiner Comments

- Point 4 is set up as a comparison to points 1, 2 and 3, although really Hugo's gentleness has no point of comparison to Jack's resilience, strength, or leadership qualities. However, the structure of point 4 does pretend to be a comparison. **1 mark.**
- Both parts of the comparison include an explanation. **1 mark.**
- Point 5 compares with point 7. **1 mark.**
- Both points contain an explanation. **1 mark.**
- Point 6 is an excellent new point, but nothing about Jack and Ben's relationship later compares with it. **Zero marks.**
- Point 10 about Hugo is a contrast to both points 8 and 9 about Jack. There was an opportunity to write a further contrast with Hugo, but the student didn't do this. So these only score **1 mark.**
- Both parts of the comparison include an explanation. **1 mark.**
- Point 11 makes a new comparison. Hugo's strength is a comparison to point 1. His bravery is a comparison to point 8. Unfortunately, this is a brilliant comparison of a similarity, rather than a ***difference***. At this stage: **Zero marks.**
- Both parts of the comparison include an explanation. **1 mark**.
- Point 12 is a conclusion. You don't need to write a conclusion. However, this point also introduces a new difference between 'gentle' Hugo and 'focused' Jack. This is a ***difference*** in how they used their strength from Point 11. So, at last: **1 mark.**
- In the real exam, this answer took the student 333 words to write. Using the Salles Method would have allowed them to score 8/8 in far fewer words. And it would be much easier to grade!

Based on AQA Paper 2 November 2019

Source A

Gregory Efimovich was a Russian writer who began a career in Mongolia 2002 as a peace keeper. At this time, Mongolia was struggling for independence from Russia and China. This extract is from his memoir, Exploding the Whale, written in 2021.

Just after dawn, the duty officer in the neighbouring town called on the telephone and said the mammoth was wrecking the market. Could I kindly come and deal with it? I had no experience in dealing with mammoths, but I was curious to see the spectacle and destruction so I set off. I took my pistol, far too tiny to stop a mammoth, but I reasoned the shots might scare it away.

Of course this was no wild mammoth, but a privately owned, genetically engineered one. It had been enclosed in a mammoth reserve, but had escaped. At dusk, the mammoth had arrived suddenly on the outskirts. Then it had flattened several huts, killed two yaks and plundered several market stalls to scoff their fruit and vegetables.

Several Mongolian horsemen rode up to tell us the mammoth was in the allotments by the river, less than a kilometre away. I sent my underling to borrow a machine gun. She returned shortly with a Makarov machine gun, with only six bullets in the chamber.

As I walked towards the river the entire town flooded from their homes to see what would happen. Rumours that I had a machine gun got them excited and another rumour that I would shoot the mammoth spread quickly. I was unhappy about this. I had no plans to shoot the mammoth. I jogged downhill, feeling like an idiot, cradling the Makarov with a horde of citizens running behind me in ranks.

At the allotments, the mammoth grazed a few meters from the path. He ignored us. He was ripping through the vegetables, brushing them against his fur to loosen the dirt, and cramming them into his jaws.

The moment I saw the mammoth I was certain I couldn't kill him. It was almost insane to kill a rare mammoth – it is like burning the Mona Lisa to keep warm. From where we stood watching it, carefully sifting its food, the mammoth looked as peaceful as a horse. I intended to watch him for half an hour and, if he did not go on a rampage, I would then return to the town.

But then I looked back at the ranks behind me. They were an army of more than a thousand, and would soon double in number. I scanned the bobbing heads and eager expressions – eyes bright with anticipation of a spectacle, everyone convinced I would kill the mammoth. They waited for me to perform like a boxer in the ring.

Now I understood I would have to execute the mammoth. The crowd were waiting for it, so I dare not disappoint. Because I represented Russia, a ruler with a machine gun, the main heavyweight fighting on the bill, though in truth I was just a blunt weapon being wielded by the mob. To have run down here, clutching the Makarov, thousands of people expecting gunfire, and not fire a shot – well, that was not going to work. They would lose respect for me.

Yet I didn't want to kill the mammoth. It would feel like murder. (Especially as the mammoth was such a rare creature).

I knew exactly what I must do. I must walk towards the mammoth to see how it reacted. If he charged me I would have to fire. If he ignored me, I could let him be. But there was no way I could risk that. If he charged, would my six bullets stop him before he ploughed through me like a cartoon villain tied to a railway track?

This vision of over a thousand Mongolians watching me being chased, trampled and snapped filled my mind. And the most likely reaction would not be horror, but laughter. That could not be allowed to happen. I had no choice.

Source B

This extract is from the book Miracles in Extinction Reversal, published in 2018 by Dr. Sergey Primov, chief geneticist at Reincarnate and Reimagine, in Siberia, Russia.

The first mammoth I genetically engineered was the famous Manfred. This Siberian woolly mammoth was created from DNA kept in permafrost for 10,000 years and an Indian elephant mother on the 12th of July 1999. We moved him to The Tundra Experience Theme Park when he was one year old, and he was raised by Dolf Lundgrun.

The first action was to train him to be around people. This required more than a little organisation. The infant creature had had little contact with humans, but by constant exposure, and varying the kinds of people he met, his socialisation was radically improved.

However, he quickly learned some very energetic and dangerous behaviours, which he thought were playful, to the extent where we had to curb his enthusiasms, and this was achieved by applying science and pain. Lundgrun and I implanted electrodes in each of his ears, through which to electrocute him. He soon realised we were his masters and lay flat and howled to indicate his submission.

We conditioned him by offering him foods as a reward, and the three of us were soon inseparable, and this continued to the very day we sold him. By the time he was eighteen he had attained the incredible height of 13 ft. Every male mammoth over eighteen begins to want to assert their dominance in the herd through violence. Manfred was a typical male in this respect.

He butchered the wooden parts of his home, splintering doors and gates, and drove his enormous tusks through the metal bars of his enclosure, twisting and bending them with ease. When his passions were roused in this way inside his house, none of his other handlers dared to approach him; yet astonishingly, once allowed his freedom outside in the Tundra Park grounds, he was completely calm.

We discovered we could curb his manic and frenetic displays of violence by limiting his food, or with gentle use of the electrodes and, on occasion, paralysing electrocution; however, this solution would alarm and draw complaints from the scientific community, and we had no desire to become front page news for our cruel and inhumane treatment of animals.

Of course, these are the ignorant views of people who have never had to dominate a six tonne male, because to fail to control such a monster would be to put your very life in danger of the mammoth's extraordinary power.

In Manfred's youth he was soon tall enough to offer rides to children and consequently a special saddle was fashioned for him. In those days, all the earnings for these rides were the property of the handler. So one can only imagine that Lundgren earned a pretty penny, especially as Manny was by far the favoured mammoth.

For his first seventeen years, Manny had been placid, good natured and easy to control, and each day hundreds of children would ride him in the Park. Now discovering in his eighteenth year that he would probably kill or maim a child, I applied to the company directors to be given a lethal enough weapon in case I needed to exterminate him.

But in the same period I was sent a request from Mr Tom Cruise to ask if I would sell 'Manny the Mammoth' to his film company Cruise Control. I replied within the hour informing Mr Cruise that the price was twenty million pounds.

Question 2

You need to refer to Source A **and** Source B for this question.

Both sources describe encounters with woolly mammoths.

Use details from **both** sources to write a summary of how the mammoths behave in similar ways.

My Response 1

1. The mammoth in Source A was not a tame animal. It "had been in a mammoth reserve, but had escaped".

2. The mammoth had "flattened several huts, killed two yaks and plundered several market stalls to scoff their fruit and vegetables".

3. But it hadn't yet threatened the lives of any people.

1 mark

Examiner Comments

- There are no comparisons. **Zero marks**.
- There are two explanations. **1 mark**.
- This generosity wouldn't necessarily apply higher up the mark bands, but all the student has to prove is that they have "simple" and "limited" understanding.

My Response 2

1. The mammoths in both sources behave in similar ways.

2. In Source A "He was ripping through the vegetables".

3. Similarly in Source B the mammoth "butchered the wooden parts of his home, splintering doors and gates".

4. **This reveals how both mammoths are destructive and behave in wild ways.**

2 marks

Examiner Comments

- Point 1 is an introduction, not a comparison or explanation. **Zero marks.**
- Points 2 and 3 are a comparison. **1 mark.**
- Both points are explained in point 4. **1 mark.**

My Response 3

1. The mammoth in Source A "was wrecking the market."

2. This implies that the animal wanted food and was playful. Perhaps he needed room because there wasn't much on the "mammoth reserve".

3. We can infer that the mammoth was playful because "the mammoth looked as peaceful as a horse".

4. In source B the mammoth behaved in a similar way. It had also **"learned some very energetic and dangerous behaviours".** *Consequently, this mammoth gets punished.*

5. We can also infer that this mammoth didn't intend to be dangerous, he actually **"thought"** his behaviours **"were playful".**

3 marks

Examiner Comments

- Point 1 is compared to point 4. **1 mark**.
- Points 2 and 4 contain the explanations. **1 mark**.
- Point 3 and 5 looks like a good comparison, but the evidence of the mammoth looking "peaceful" doesn't really prove that it is playful. So this is not a real comparison. **Zero marks**.
- Point 5 does include an explanation matched to a valid point. This is worth half a mark which, as you know can't be awarded. The examiner asks, has the answer moved from "simple" and "limited" to "some"? If so, the half can be rounded up. **1 mark.**

My Response 4

1. *The behaviour of the mammoth in Source A was violent*: "it had flattened several huts".

2. *It is also very dangerous* because it "killed two yaks".

3. *This might be a reaction to having been cooped up in the reserve.*

4. *The mammoth in Source B was also violent* as he "drove his enormous tusks through the metal bars of his enclosure".

5. *This implies the mammoth had not been tamed while in the Park.*

6. *The behaviours mean that both mammoths are likely to be shot.*

4 marks

Examiner Comments

- Point 1 compares with point 4. **1 mark.**
- Both points include an explanation. **1 mark.**
- Point 2 is just about compared to point 6. **1 mark.**
- Both points include an explanation. **1 mark.**

- Point 3 is not a new comparison. It is only an extra explanation to point 2, which already includes an explanation. **Zero marks.**

My Response 5

1. The mammoth in Source A destroys property: "it had flattened several huts".

2. One cause of this behaviour might be that it felt trapped because "It had been enclosed in a mammoth reserve".

3. The mammoth in Source B also destroys property, when "He butchered the wooden parts of his home, splintering doors and gates".

4. This suggests that he has become angered, feeling trapped in his enclosure and denied freedom.

5. In Source A, the escaped mammoth appears to have calmed down, "carefully sifting its food, the mammoth looked as peaceful as a horse".

6. In Source B, the mammoth has been made peaceful by being released from the enclosure, "once allowed his freedom outside in the Tundra Park grounds, he was completely calm".

7. This implies that the mammoth responds to being treated humanely, rather than simply being tamed through electrocution.

5 marks

Examiner Comments

- Points 1 and point 3 are a comparison. **1 mark.**
- Points 2 and 4 explain this comparison. **1 mark.**
- Points 5 and 6 are a comparison. **1 mark.**
- Both include an explanation. **1 mark.**
- Point 7 is the beginning of a new comparison and a new explanation. Half marks can't be awarded. 4 marks would mean the answer as a whole showed only "some attempts" at comparison. 5 marks is 'clear and relevant'. The examiner decides on the latter. **1 mark.**
- If you follow the Salles Method, you can see that the *only* way to end up with an odd number of marks is if you don't complete a comparison with explanations. So, you might write a comparison with no explanation – that would give an odd mark. Or you might write half a comparison with an explanation. Then the examiner will look at the grade descriptor and ask if it puts your answer into the next band.

My Response 6

1. The mammoth in Source A "had flattened several huts, killed two yaks and plundered several market stalls to scoff their fruit and vegetables" once it had escaped from the reserve.

2. Similarly, the mammoth in Source B *also became destructive after escaping its enclosure*, "He butchered the wooden parts of his home, splintering doors and gates".

3. *Consequently, both mammoths became violent after their escapes from their keepers.*

4. Their behaviour after escaping is also similar, *because they both became calmer following their destructive behaviours.*

5. The mammoth in Source A is described as "carefully sifting its food, the mammoth looked as peaceful as a horse" after its rampage.

6. In Source B the mammoth is similarly described as "once allowed his freedom outside in the Tundra Park grounds, he was completely calm."

5 marks

Examiner Comments

- Points 1 and 2 are a comparison. **1 mark.**
- Point 3 contains explanations for both points 1 and 2. **1 mark.**
- Point 3 also tells us a new comparison, not just what the behaviour is after escaping, but as a result of escaping their handlers. Although this comparison is made very briefly, it is still a comparison. **1 mark.**
- There is no explanation as to why escaping their handlers have made become violent – so no extra marks for an explanation. **Zero marks.**
- Points 5 and 6 are a new comparison. **1 mark.**
- Both points are explained in point 4. **1 mark.**

My Response 7

1. The mammoth in Source A, "had flattened several huts, killed two yaks and plundered several market stalls".

2. *We can infer from this that the mammoth in Source A has probably suffered from being kept in captivity*, which *has made him disobedient and destructive.*

3. The mammoth in Source B is similarly destructive, as "He butchered the wooden parts of his home, splintering doors and gates".

4. *We can infer there is a similar cause to this destruction, which is being kept captive in an enclosure.*

5. After this rampage, the mammoth in Source A acts more tamely, "carefully sifting its food, the mammoth looked as peaceful as a horse."

6. *We can infer that it is calm and unthreatening.*

7. *We can also infer that this is because the mammoth chooses its habitat.*

8. The mammoth in Source B also becomes unthreatening when he is released from his enclosure, "Manny had been placid, good natured and easy to control".

9. We can infer that this mammoth also becomes tamer.

10. We can infer that this also only happens when, like the mammoth in Source A, it has more choice over its habitat.

6 marks

Examiner Comments

- Point 1 compares with point 3. **1 mark.**
- Points 2 and 4 contain explanations. **1 mark.**
- Point 5 compares with point 8. **1 mark.**
- Points 6 and 9 contain explanations of this comparison. **1 mark.**
- Points 7 and 10 are a further comparison. **1 mark.**
- They each contain an explanation. **1 mark.**
- Once again, you can see how the comparisons are all over the place, and it would be much easier for the examiner to mark if it was organised with the Salles Method.
- More importantly this student would clearly see that they had only 3 comparisons, and so would need to find another one. After writing this answer, the student has no clue what sort of mark it might get.

My Response 8

1. The mammoth in Source A had previously been "no wild animal" ***and presumably peaceful.***

2. The mammoth in Source B had similarly been "placid, good natured and easy to control".

3. ***Both mammoths then became destructive overnight.*** In Source A after it had escaped, and in Source B as soon as it turned "eighteen".

4. The mammoth in Source A is so destructive that "it had flattened several huts, killed two yaks".

5. This is similar to the mammoth in Source B which become so violent "that he would probably kill or maim a child".

6. The destructive behaviour in Source A ***is caused by the mammoth simply wanting to eat***, "From where we stood watching it, carefully sifting its food".

7. ***We can tell that it does not mean to be harmful as***, while eating, "the mammoth looked as peaceful as a horse".

8. ***The misbehaviour of the mammoth in Source B is also related to food***, so that "we could curb his manic and frenetic displays of violence by limiting his food".

9. This mistreatment and the "paralysing electrocution" ***probably explain why the mammoth in Source B wanted to escape its handlers.***

10. ***This is possibly similar to the mammoth in Source A which has clearly escaped in order to get more food, from which we can infer it was mistreated and not fed properly in the reserve.***

7 marks

Examiner Comments

- Point 1 compares with point 2. **1 mark.**
- There is only one explanation in point 1, and none in point 2. Half marks can't be awarded. **Zero marks.**
- Point 3 compares both sources in the same point. **1 mark.**
- Point 3 also includes an explanation for both sources. **1 mark.**
- Point 4 compares with point 5. **1 mark.**
- There is no explanation in points 4 and 5. **Zero marks.**
- Point 6 compares to point 8. **1 mark.**
- Both points include an explanation. **1 mark.**
- Point 7 introduces a new comparison, with an explanation, but this isn't followed up with a comparison to Source B. The examiner can't award half marks, and the answer is already in the top band. **Zero marks.**
- Point 9 compares with point 10. **1 mark.**
- Both points contain an explanation. The examiner has probably decided that there is no evidence for the explanation in point 10, and therefore decided it can't be "perceptive". **Zero marks.**

My Response 9

1. The mammoth in Source A *behaves in a destructive way*, "wrecking the market", and "had flattened several huts, killed two yaks and plundered several market stalls".

2. This is similar *to the destructive behaviour of the mammoth* in Source B who "butchered the wooden parts of his home, splintering doors and gates".

3. The level of destruction in both sources suggests that they have become potentially dangerous to people.

4. We can tell that the behaviour is dangerous in Source A because the mammoth had already "killed two yaks" *and Efimovich decided he needed a* "machine gun".

5. Similarly, in Source B, *the mammoth was so dangerous* "none of his other handlers dared to approach him" *and there was a risk* "he would probably kill or maim a child" *and so Dr. Zimov wanted a* "lethal weapon".

6. Once the mammoth in Source A has escaped, *he appears quite tame*, "carefully sifting its food, the mammoth looked as peaceful as a horse".

7. *This is similar to Source B*, where the mammoth is released from its enclosure into the Park, and "once allowed his freedom outside in the Tundra Park grounds, he was completely calm".

8. *It is probable that both mammoths behave this way in response to their mistreatment.* In Source B the mammoth has been "electrocuted" and pent up in an "enclosure" with "metal bars".

9. Similarly, in Source A, the reserve had "enclosed" the mammoth *so it felt the need to escape.*

10. *The mammoth in Source A doesn't seem to pose a danger to the public. Even though there are a huge number of people*, over a "thousand", the mammoth "ignored us".

11. *The mammoth in Source B also doesn't seem to pose an immediate threat to the public,* "once allowed his freedom outside in the Tundra Park grounds, he was completely calm" *and at the minute only threatens his handlers in his enclosure.*

Examiner Comments

- Point 1 compares to point 2. **1 mark.**
- Both points include an explanation. **1 mark.**
- Point 3 compares the mammoth's behaviour in both sources, using the same evidence as point 1 and 2. 1 mark. This is quite high risk though, as it doesn't use a separate quotation or evidence. So, let's call it **zero marks**.
- Point 3 includes an explanation. 1 mark. But, as above, the examiner could say this is just a deeper explanation of similar evidence, so **no extra mark**.
- Point 4 compares with point 5. **1 mark.**
- Both points include an explanation. **1 mark.**
- Point 6 compares to point 7. **1 mark.**
- Both include an explanation. **1 mark.**
- Point 8 compares to point 9. **1 mark.**
- Both points include an explanation. **1 mark.**
- Up to this point is enough for 8 marks.
- I wrote this answer because I'm curious to see if the examiners choose texts where you don't have to spot 100% of the differences or similarities to get 8 marks. The good news is that there is one more comparison we could make:
- Point 10 compares to point 11. **1 mark.**
- Both points include an explanation. **1 mark.**

The total is capped at 8 marks. So, you need to find 4 out of the 5 comparisons in the texts to get full marks.

Printed in Great Britain
by Amazon

25594231R00024